This book is dedicated to c
Cats express their opinions in a variety of ways and
with a cat, we usually know exactly what the opinion is.

No part of this book may be reproduced in any form by any electronic or
mechanical means including photocopying, recording, or information storage
and retrieval without permission from Marian Brickner and Linda Whitefeather.

In the quiet
Of each dark night
A symphony
Of motion, light

Cat knows the path
From bed to bowl
Silently takes
His nightly stroll

Leaves camouflage
An almond stare
Quickly turning
Into a glare

Being spotted
He knows no shame
By finding him
You are to blame

Cat has found his
Forever home
With simple fix
He will not roam

But grow happy,
Old and content
On soft carpet
Not hard cement

Look! Look right here!
I spot a spot!
Do you see it?
A small red dot!

How can it be
A simple toy
Can bring a cat
Such endless joy?

Another piece
Goes pop, pop, pop
Plastic bubbles
Oh, make it stop!

The little cat
From Peoria
Has found his joy
His euphoria

Got the jumpies?
No, nothing's wrong!
As 'cat I must
Go sprong, sprong, sprong!

Down the hallway
Across the room
Bounce the window
Then zoom, zoom, zoom!

From the window
Then thru the door
Cat swaggers out
Life to explore

Cat is stillness
'Til birds tweet, tweet
Then he's moving
Up, down the street

Is that a bird?
Stuck in your mouth!
Open up now!
And let it out!

Little birdie
Lost a feather
So he's feeling
Under weather

A cat in rage
Knows how to sulk
And make light fur
Substantial bulk

Make no mistake
'Bout big, puffy
This cat is not
Sweet and fluffy

You keep asking
That I say "cheese"
Best you say it
With "pretty please"

I am a cat
My smile appears
Not on my lips
But eyes and ears

This may surprise
It may astound
There are some cats
Who make no sound

For they have deigned
The human herd
A subspecies
Below the bird

Can-open-man
The time is now
For you to make
My bowl of chow

So get moving
This tail will twirl
Until I hear
That can go whirl

Kitty, kitty
Come over here
Let me scratch you
Behind an ear

Hear me, kitty
Why won't you come?
Oh don't pretend
That you are dumb

Ears flat back lay
Eyes all squinty
These my weapons
Sharp and flinty

Yet claws and teeth
You must beware
Mass destruction
Extraordinaire!

I am a cat
Not a sonnet
Though I wear a
Silly bonnet

Thank my human's
Little grandchild
Who's gone outside
Still running wild

"Forever home?"
Is this my place?
My very own
Personal space?

Can I trust you?
Will you keep me
No matter if
Your bed I pee?

I am kitten
Hear me roaring
A companion
Never boring

When I grow up
I will be CAT!
And rule your life
Get used to THAT!

Look! Look at me!
Look at me now!
Aren't I pretty?
So lovely? Wow!

Grooming hourly
Is my routine
Until - lick, lick -
I am pristine

No, I'm not sick
The summer breeze
Carries odors
That make me sneeze

Let the window
Be open wide
So I can smell
The things outside

39

Hello Friends

We had a lot of fun creating this book of poems about cats.
"So remember, you're nobody until you've been ignored by a cat." (Linda)

The cats were not asked to do anything particular, but were photographed
just being themselves. Although I have a personal ban against
photoshopping my work, I DID add the hat to the cat on page 31
in order to fulfill the intent of the poem. (Marian)

We can be reached at the following:

Linda Whitefeather
catfeather32301@gmail.com

Marian Brickner
insect1@att.net
www.marianbricknerphotography.com

c
a
t
s

40

Books by Marian

Cat Books

Lexi My Cat
Cat Portraits
Cats

Dog Books
Barnhunt
Dogs of Circle Lake
Dog Portraits
With Bright Shiny Faces
Seasoned Dogs

Books for Fun
Go Fish!
What are they thinking?
What's a Family Anyway?
Mutts and Rascals
Animals Don't Wear Lipstick
Subliminal Nuances
of Animal Behavior

Bonobo Books

Lorel (mom age 36) and Lucy (age 1)

I'm Lucy, A Day in the Life
of a Young Bonobo
Is Lucy Singing?
Grooming Bonobos Lucy Loves It
Growing up Bonobo
Bonobo Lucy Grows up
Bonobo Lucy and her baby Yuli

Empathy Books
Insides out
You Scared me
I'm Different -You're Different

©Marian Brickner

Made in the USA
Middletown, DE
06 December 2022

17337685R00024